# Understanding
# My Lizard

Reptiles are becoming very popular pets and are overtaking cats and dogs as household members, however, their husbandry requirements are much more complex to keep them happy and healthy.

As a company who sees every day the shortfalls in caring for these specialised animals, we are pleased to endorse the series of "Reptiles are Cool" written by Siuna Reid, an experienced exotic veterinarian who cares enough to try and make a difference.

These books are very basic and provide simple steps and explanations of how and why we need to provide specialised environments for our pet reptiles to improve their captive quality of life as best we can.

—Pinmoore Animal Laboratory Services

REPTILES ARE COOL

# Understanding
# My Lizard

## Siuna A Reid
BVMS Cert AVP (ZM) MRCVS

Edited by
Vivienne E Lodge

**Copyright © 2013 by Siuna Ann Reid**

The right of Siuna Ann Reid to be identified as the author of this work has been asserted by her in accordance with the Copyright, Designs and Patents Act 1988.

This edition published in 2013 by Siuna Ann Reid.

ISBN 978-0-9576568-3-3

All rights reserved. Apart from any use permitted under UK copyright law, this publication may not be reproduced, stored or transmitted by any means, without prior permission of the copyright holder.

The guidelines in this book cannot guarantee a healthy lizard. The author takes no responsibility for any subsequent illness or death.

Whilst every effort has been made to ensure that the information contained within this book is correct at the time of going to press, the author and publisher can take no responsibility for the errors or omissions contained within.

Printed in the Great Britain by Lightning Source UK
Book and Cover Design by www.wordzworth.com

**To Mum**

I love you.

# CONTENTS

| | |
|---|---|
| INTRODUCTION | 1 |
| LIZARDS AS PETS | 3 |
| VISITING THE VET | 5 |
| THE HOUSE | 6 |
| SUBSTRATE & FURNITURE | 7 |
| HEAT AND LIGHT | 8 |
| ULTRA VIOLET LIGHT | 10 |
| WATER | 11 |
| FOOD | 12 |
| SKIN | 14 |
| EYES | 22 |
| DIGESTIVE SYSTEM | 26 |
| LUNGS | 33 |
| HEART | 35 |
| REPRODUCTIVE SYSTEM | 37 |
| KIDNEYS | 42 |
| NUTRITIONAL DISEASE | 47 |
| PARASITES | 51 |
| GROWTHS, TRAUMA & AUTOTOMY | 53 |
| NEUROLOGICAL DISEASE | 56 |
| INDEX | 58 |

Siuna A Reid

# INTRODUCTION

I have been a vet for a long time and I have seen many changes in the kinds of animals that I treat. Over the past ten years there has been a huge increase in the number of reptiles that are kept as pets.

Reptiles are very different from mammals. The purpose of this book is to try to explain these differences and why they are important to the health and wellbeing of pet reptiles.

There are hundreds of different species of lizards being kept as pets. The onus is on the supervising adult to research the specific requirements before buying their pet. This book explains the importance of husbandry and some of the diseases that can occur if basic needs are not fulfilled.

Reptiles carry many different bacteria, one of which is salmonella. Although not harmful to them, the bacteria can cause illness in humans. Therefore, it is essential to wash your hands thoroughly after handling all reptiles.

There are two species of venomous lizard. These are the Beaded Lizard and the Gia Monster. Both require a zoo license to keep and are not suitable as pets.

Later in the book you will come across the following symbols. Each one highlights a particular aspect of your reptile's care, relating directly to the health issue being discussed.

  House

  Furniture

  Heat and Light

  UV light

  Water/Humidity

  Food

# LIZARDS AS PETS

Buying a pet and looking after it is a huge responsibility. As a pet owner you have to make sure that your pet has somewhere suitable to live, has the correct food to eat and receives lots of care and attention. You have to notice when your pet is not feeling well and may need to be taken to the vet.

The most commonly kept pets are mammals such as dogs, cats, rabbits and hamsters. Humans are mammals too, so we generally find it quite easy to relate to other mammals and to realise when they are unwell or in distress. If you stand on your dog's paw he will yelp and you will know he is in pain. If your dog is too cold you will notice that he is shivering and if he is too hot you will notice that he is panting. If he doesn't eat his dinner you will realise that he is feeling unwell.

You have chosen to keep a lizard as a pet. Lizards are reptiles and reptiles are very different from mammals. Your lizard will not give you such obvious signals to let you know that he is feeling unwell, or too hot, or too cold, or in pain. His signs of distress are much more subtle and you will have to observe him very closely to make sure that he is healthy otherwise his suffering will go unnoticed. You should weigh your lizard regularly as it may not be obvious just from looking at him that he is losing weight.

Many of the health problems which occur in lizards are related to some aspect of their environment or their diet. In this book we will first look at the correct housing and feeding for your lizard. Then we will go through the body systems of your lizard to find out how they work and what to look out for should things go wrong.

## CAPTIVE BRED

Wherever possible buy a captive bred lizard. Lizards bought from wild stock are often exposed to, and can carry a wide range of different parasites, bacteria and viruses. Buying a wild caught lizard also encourages this unethical trade.

## HOLIDAY CARE

Everybody needs a holiday! When choosing a suitable place for your lizard to stay whilst you are away, ensure that he is not exposed to other lizards. If your lizard is either living in isolation, or in an isolated group, suddenly placing him in an environment where there are other lizards could be dangerous. There is a huge risk of disease spread. Wherever possible, arrange for your lizard to be cared for at your own home.

## INSURANCE

Please note that lizard health care is specialised and should they become ill treatment can be expensive. Insurance is one way to help towards the cost of veterinary care.

# VISITING THE VET

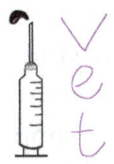

At some point you may need to take your lizard to the vet. This symbol, which you will come across throughout the book, indicates when you will need to seek extra help, medicine or maybe even surgery for your lizard. Try to choose a vet who has a special interest in reptiles. Some vets take more exams so that they have extra qualifications for treating reptiles. If your local vets are not reptile enthusiasts they should be able to recommend a vet who is. If you have difficulty finding a suitable vet you could contact The Royal College of Veterinary Surgeons www.rcvs.org.uk.

# THE HOUSE

 Where will your lizard live? You will need to buy a tank for him to use as his house. It is best to get the tank (and also the things that you put in it – see below) from a specialist reptile shop. Tanks made of glass or plastic are a good idea as these materials are easy to clean.

Within the tank you are trying to create a small world which mimics the kind of environment that your species of lizard would live in if it were living in the wild. Desert species, such as the Bearded Dragon, need a dry environment. Tropical species, such as the iguana, thrive in more humid surroundings. Therefore it is very important that you fully research your chosen species so that you can create the correct living environment.

It is also important to think about where within your home you will place the lizard's house. The best place is within a room that is used, like your bedroom or the main living room. Your lizard needs to be somewhere with a constant temperature. Do not put his house beside a window or over a radiator as the temperature will rise and fall too much in these areas.

# SUBSTRATE & FURNITURE

 Substrate is the material used to cover the floor of your lizard's house. If you have a desert species you should provide him with sand. A tropical species needs a combination of soil and moss.

You will also need to put some furniture in his house. He needs to have somewhere to hide, especially if his house is in a busy room. You can buy him a plastic cave or you can use pieces of wood or log to make a hide. Plants such as vines can also be used for making hiding areas. Natural plants look good in a tank, but it is also possible to use plastic ones which have the added advantage of being easy to clean.

# HEAT AND LIGHT

 Life on Earth is supported by the sun. The sun provides heat and also light. Animals' need both heat and light to survive.

Mammals can control their own body temperature. The food they eat provides the body with energy and heat. If they are too cold they shiver and if they are too hot they sweat. These processes use up a lot of energy.

Your lizard is a reptile and reptiles regulate their body temperature very differently from mammals. This is a major and vitally important difference. Reptiles are cold blooded (exothermic). This means that their bodies cannot produce heat from the food that they eat. Because of this they need

 much less energy from food to survive. A 100g reptile needs only 5% of the energy that a 100g mammal needs. To keep warm they need to bathe in the sun or sit on a warm

rock. They have no hair, no sweat glands and do not shiver. This means that your lizard will show no obvious signs that they are too hot or too cold.

You need to provide sources of heat for your lizard within his house. This could be a heat bulb, a hot rock or an under floor heating mat. It is important that you know the temperature in your lizard's house, both the hottest and the coolest areas. To do this you will need to use thermometers to check all around their house. A thermostat is a device that should be added to the house to control the temperature.

If you are not aware of the temperature in your lizard's house there is a danger that he could become too hot. As he cannot sweat to cool off, or remove layers of clothing as we would, he will need to try to hide in a cooler part of his tank. Providing a water bath is a good idea.

It is more common, however, for a lizard to find himself in an environment which is too cold. Cooler temperatures are unlikely to kill him, but will put a strain on his body and organs. His muscles, lungs, intestines and heart will struggle to work if they are too cold, and if this goes on for a long time it can lead to illness and even death.

# ULTRA VIOLET LIGHT

 As well as producing heat and light, the sun also produces ultraviolet (UV) light. This is a type of light which we cannot see but lizards can. It affects the skin and in humans it can cause sunburn.

Reptiles use UV light to make vitamin D3. This helps to keep their bones strong and healthy and enables their guts to absorb calcium from their food. To obtain vitamin D3 he will need exposure to UV light for 12 hours a day.

If your lizard does not receive enough vitamin D3 his bones will become soft and they may even snap and break. He may develop twitchy toes caused by faulty muscle contractions.

Ultra violet light can be provided as a combination bulb or a UV tube. The tube needs to be no more than 30cm away from your lizard. Remember that a UV tube will not provide him with any heat. The bulb should be changed once a year. Although the bulb may appear to be working, over time it will eventually stop making UV light.

# WATER

All lizards need water to drink. It is important that it is clean and regularly changed. Without water his body will become dehydrated. Dehydration can lead to constipation. If your lizard becomes constipated he could die.

Humidity is also an important consideration when setting up your lizard's house. When water evaporates it forms an invisible gas called water vapour. Humidity is a measure of the amount of water vapour that is present in the air.

In hot dry areas, like deserts, there is not a lot of water vapour in the air which means that deserts have low humidity. Rain forests are also hot but they have lots of water vapour in the air and so they have high humidity.

The level of humidity required for your lizard will depend on what type of lizard he is and therefore what type of environment he needs to live in. You can use a gadget called a hygrometer to measure the level of humidity in your lizard's house to ensure that it is suitable for him.

# FOOD

The diet of lizards will differ depending on where they are from. Lizards like iguanas are herbivorous, eating plants and leaves. Other lizards like the Bearded Dragon eat insects when they are young and developing but change to a diet with more salad and greens as they mature. Many of the large lizards like the Monitors are omnivorous. This means that they eat meat, eggs, fish, insects and leaves. In the wild a lizard would eat whatever types of insects he could catch, depending on the season. In captivity you will have to buy live insects for him to eat.

Most of the insects that are fed to pet lizards are mass reared. Traditionally, locusts, black and brown crickets, meal worms and wax worms have been used. Mario worms and calci worms can also be obtained. This is a very artificial situation and we are greatly simplifying our geckos' diets by offering them such a limited variety of insects.

All insects are very low in vitamins and minerals. When you buy your crickets or other insects from the supplier, they are often hungry and have eaten part of their cardboard containers. This further reduces their mineral content. You can boost the mineral levels by feeding some dry fish flakes or small amounts of greens, such as dandelions to your live food. Dusting the insects with calcium/vitamin D3 powder before feeding them to your lizard will also help. This will ensure that he receives adequate amounts of these minerals in his diet.

Don't be afraid to catch other insects, for example moths, or spiders to feed to your lizard. These will be packed full of nutrients and will be better for him than the commercially produced live food. If you catch insects from your garden make sure that it hasn't been treated with chemicals.

The frequency with which you feed your lizard will depend on his age and stage of development. It is important not to put too many live insects into his house at one time. Some of them might bite his skin, which will cause pain and damage. They can also annoy your lizard causing him to become agitated and unhappy. So if he is not hungry, take the live food out and try again later. There is nothing worse than having your dinner sitting on your head!

# SKIN

The skin is the largest organ of the body. Reptile skin is unique and has many functions which include protecting the body, providing camouflage and making vitamin D3.

## SHEDDING (ECDYSIS)

When mammals grow, their skin stretches and grows too. Reptiles are different. Their skin does not stretch with growth. Therefore, the ability to shed skin is very important to your lizard. When it is time to shed, your lizard will produce a chemical which divides the old and the new skin. At this stage his skin will look dull and bluish. He will naturally rub himself against rough or moist furniture to remove his old skin in large pieces. You will now see his shiny and colourful new skin.

It is important to keep a diary of how often your lizard sheds.

## DYSECDYSIS

Sometimes lizards have problems shedding. This is known as dysecdysis. It is one of the most common reasons for visiting the vet.

Make sure that the temperature in your lizard's house is correct. If it is too cold he will struggle to shed.

Lack of humidity is one of the most common reasons for failure to shed. You can increase the humidity by spraying the tank with water. Just make sure it is not too wet as this can lead to ulcers on the skin.

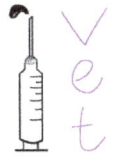
Any problems relating to shedding should be closely monitored and may require a visit to the vet.

# SKIN PROBLEMS

## ABSCESSES

Abscesses are lumps on the skin infected with bacteria or fungi. Damaged skin is a common cause of infection.

Check for sharp objects in the house.

Correct temperature will help your lizard fight off infection

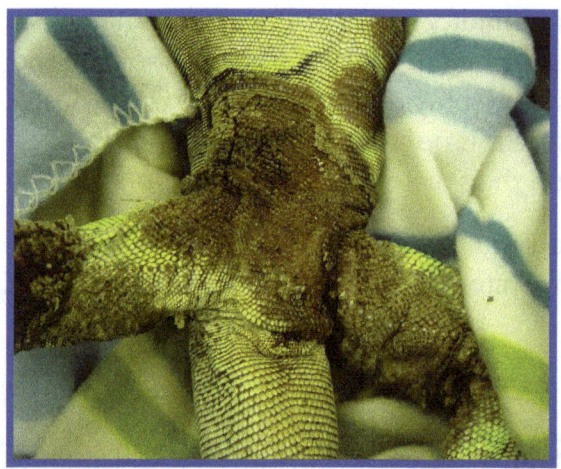

 A good diet keeps the immune system healthy.

 Make sure the furniture has smooth edges.

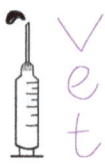 If your lizard does develops an abscess he will need to have an operation to remove it. Fungal infections are very difficult to treat. A considerable amount of medicine may be needed to cure any disease.

## BURNS

Thermal burns happen when lizards come into contact with an unprotected hot surface. This could be a heat lamp or a hot rock. Lizards seem to have difficulty detecting hot surfaces and do not react until serious damage has already been done to their skin.

Always check that any bulbs, heat pads or hot rocks in your lizard's house are working properly, to prevent burning. If the heat bulb is inside the house always ensure that it has a wire cage around it.

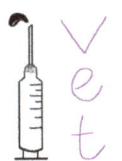

Minor burns may not need any treatment. However, serious burns will need veterinary care. This treatment may include creams and antibiotics.

17

## NUTRITIONAL SKIN DISEASE

Poor diet can affect the skin. Vitamin A is very important to lizards skin. Too little of it makes the skin of the eyes and mouth become swollen. Poor sight will make it very difficult to see and therefore feeding becomes a challenge. Too much vitamin A in the diet causes the skin to become thickened and flaky.

A diet with low calcium and low vitamin D3, but with lots of fat, can result in the body growing too quickly. This leads to weak bones and skin that sheds over and over again.

To help your lizard make vitamin D3, his UV bulb needs to have the correct strength and be placed in the correct position.

Make sure you feed a balanced diet to your lizard to ensure he gets the adequate amount of nutrients, vitamins and minerals to keep his skin healthy. Remember to feed his live food on greens and fish food flakes. Also dust the live food with a calcium supplement before feeding to your lizard.

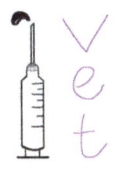 Most nutritional diseases require veterinary assistance.

## ABRASIONS (CUTS)

 Very active lizards can damage their face against the glass or plastic in the house. The damage can be serious.

 A band of cardboard, or a towel over the front of the house helps the lizard to see the glass.

 Check all the furniture for sharp edges.

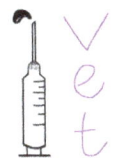 Cuts often need antibiotics and cream to help them heal.

## MITES

Look for little black or red dots on the skin. The mites breed in the house. They bite the skin which becomes very itchy. Affected lizards are often restless and will rub their face and skin.

The house will need to be cleaned thoroughly to get rid of all the mites and their eggs. Don't take your lizard to a pet shop when you go on holiday. Mites can spread very easily.

The furniture will need to be cleaned and fresh substrate placed in the house.

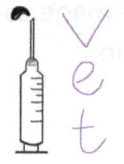

The vet will be able to give you flea medicine to kill the mites.

## GANGRENE

Gangrene is seen commonly in lizards. There are two types of gangrene, wet and dry. Dry gangrene is most common and is caused by bacteria that invade the skin and cause it to die.

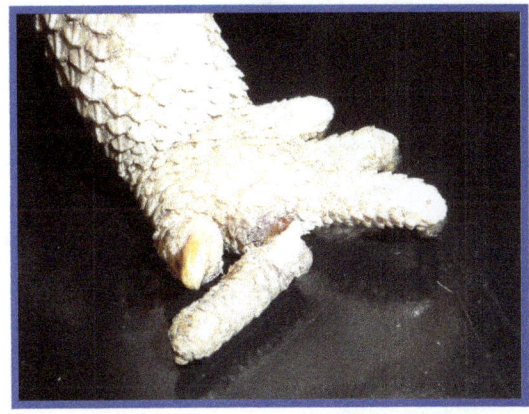

It is seen in the tail and the hands and feet. Untreated gangrene may cause your lizard to lose a toe or a whole foot.

  Make sure there are no sharp edges in the house or on the furniture which may cause cuts to the lizard. Keep an eye on any house mates to make sure they are not fighting.

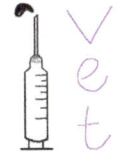 The correct temperature helps the lizard to fight infection.

 Gangrene needs surgical and medical treatment by the vet.

# EYES

Lizards have extremely good eyes that see colour and also ultra violet light.

Lizard eyelids are quite different to ours. If you look at your own eye you will see that you have a big upper eyelid which comes down to cover your eye when you blink, and a much smaller lower eyelid. In lizards the upper eyelid is smaller and the lower eyelid is bigger and stronger. Lizards also have a third eyelid which sweeps across the surface of the eye to clean it when they blink.

The coloured circle in your eye is called the iris. This deterimines whether you have green, blue or brown eyes. The pupil is in the centre of the iris. Your pupil is black and round. It can become bigger or smaller depending the amount of light around you.

Lizards have round or slit pupils depending on whether they are a species that is awake during the day or night. Often the iris is the same colour as the pattern on their skin. The iris appear as slits when they are awake at night (nocturnal). Day time lizards tend to have a round pupil. Unlike us, your lizard can move his iris if he wants to.

Lizards have tiny bones in the white part of their eyes called scleral ossicles. These help to give the eyeball extra strength.

# EYE PROBLEMS

## CONJUNCTIVITIS

Conjunctivitis is an inflammation of the eyelids. It is often caused by a bacterial infection.

Low temperatures in your lizard's house will reduce the ability to fight infection.

A balanced diet will help fight infection.

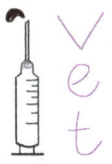
Conjunctivitis should be treated with antibiotics.

## HYPOVITAMINOSIS A

A diet lacking in vitamin A can lead to swelling of the eyelids.

Ensure that you feed a balanced diet with sufficient vitamin A to prevent eye problems with your lizard.

## TRAUMA (DAMAGE)

**Damage to the upper eyelid from a fight wound**

Any trauma to your lizard's eye could result in serious damage. This could happen in several ways. Examples would be, bedding caught in the eye or a scratch caused by a sharp object. An ulcer may form on the cornea. This is the transparent outer layer of the eye. Ulcers are very painful and in severe cases may cause the eye to burst.

  To prevent eye trauma you should check your lizard's house and furniture carefully for any sharp objects. Remember to take extra care when handling your lizard outside of his house. Cage mates can also inflict serious damage if they fight.

 Take care when selecting a UV light for your lizard's house. Inferior lights can emit harmful rays which could burn his eyes.

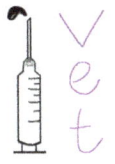 If you suspect your lizard has suffered any trauma to his eye take him to the vet immediately. Eye damage is an emergency and if not treated in time, your lizard may lose his eye.

# DIGESTIVE SYSTEM

The digestive system is the part of the body that converts food into energy. Left over waste is expelled through the vent.

The digestive tract of your lizard consists of the mouth, stomach, intestines and vent. The vent is the reptile equivalent of the anus in mammals.

## MOUTH

Lizards have lots of very small bones similar to teeth. When these break they regrow. In our mouths the roof is called the hard palate. The lizard does not have a roof to his mouth. Instead he has a hole called the choana. The tongue of the lizard varies depending on the species. Tegus have a forked tongue whilst bearded dragons have a short fleshy tongue.

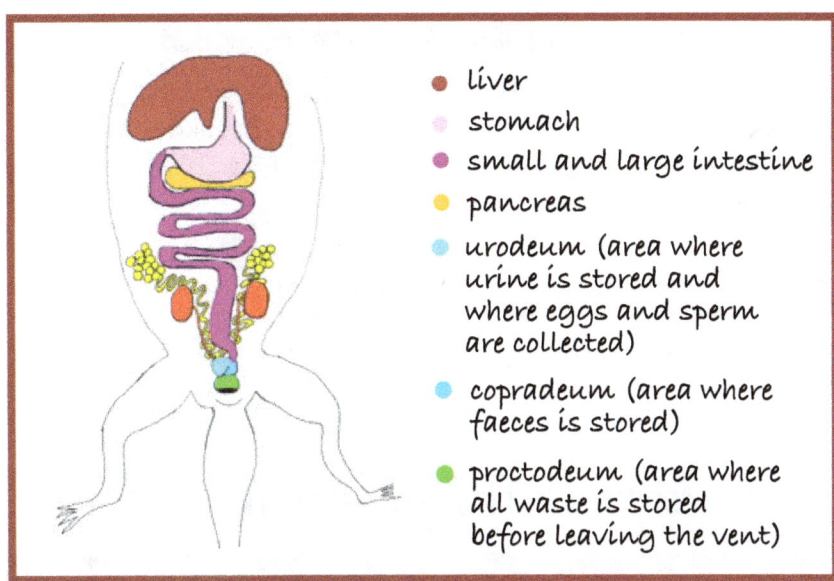

- liver
- stomach
- small and large intestine
- pancreas
- urodeum (area where urine is stored and where eggs and sperm are collected)
- copradeum (area where faeces is stored)
- proctodeum (area where all waste is stored before leaving the vent)

## STOMACH

A tube called the oesophagus leads from the mouth to the stomach.

## INTESTINES

After the stomach the digestive tract continues as the small and large intestine.

## VENT

The vent is made up of three areas. The food waste from the large intestine is stored in the coprodeum. The urodeum is the area which stores urine, and also any sperm or eggs (depending on whether your lizard is male or female). Both the coprodeum and urodeum empty into the proctodeum, and from here all faeces and urine are passed out of the vent.

## LIVER

The liver is the largest organ inside the body and has many functions. It plays an important part in the breakdown of proteins and fats from the food. It helps the body to expel any poisons and other harmful substances.

## PANCREAS

The pancreas produces juices which help to breakdown food.

# PROBLEMS OF THE DIGESTIVE SYSTEM

## STOMATITIS

Stomatitis is an inflammation of the mouth. It is commonly known as mouth rot. Stomatitis can be caused by viral or bacterial infection. It can also be caused by damage to the mouth.

Pay particular attention to the condition of the house. Very active species such as water dragons may need the glass of the house to be covered to prevent them from running at the glass or plastic front.

Low temperatures in the house can lead to a weakening of his immune system.

Check the furniture in your lizard's house to make sure that there are no sharp areas which could damage his mouth.

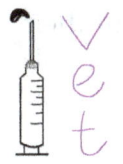
If you think your lizard might have stomatitis have him checked by the vet.

## FATTY LIVER DISEASE

Lizards need to eat regularly. Fatty liver disease is also known as hepatic lipidosis. Liver cells become swamped with fat, preventing the liver from working properly. It is very difficult to detect fatty liver disease. There are no obvious symptoms but a lizard with this condition will stop eating. It is important to weigh your lizard regularly to spot severe weight loss.

Low temperature can cause loss of appetite.

If the food for your lizard is too big, or if you feed too many insects at once, this can put him off his food. Make sure you are feeding a good balanced diet for your particular species of lizard.

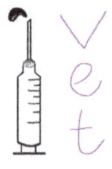
If your lizard loses more than 10% of his bodyweight you should take him to the vet.

## IMPACTION AND CONSTIPATION

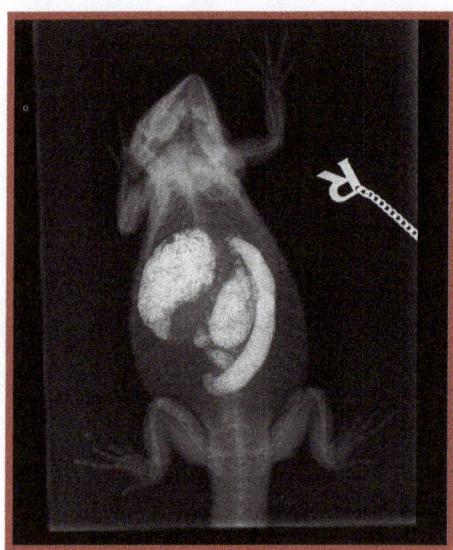

Lizards often eat material from the floor of their house by mistake. This can lead to impaction in the large intestine. This is when pieces of material clump together and cause a blockage. Constipation is when a lizard cannot pass faeces. If your lizard is constipated you might notice him straining to pass faeces or that his faeces look very dry.

The temperature in your lizard's house is vital. If it is too cold the intestines cannot digest food properly and this can lead to constipation.

Calcium is needed to make the intestines work properly. Ensure that your lizard's UV light is at the correct height and is not too old.

It is very important that your lizard has water at all times and that the humidity in his house is at the correct level. Dehydration often leads to constipation.

Be sure your lizard is eating the correct type and amount of food. If he is greedy his intestines may become too full and therefore prone to impaction.

Ensure the material you use for the floor of the tank is large enough not to be swallowed by a hungry lizard.

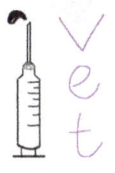
This condition is often left until it is too late. If an impaction is very severe an operation may be necessary to remove the material blocking the intestine.

## PROLAPSE OF THE VENT

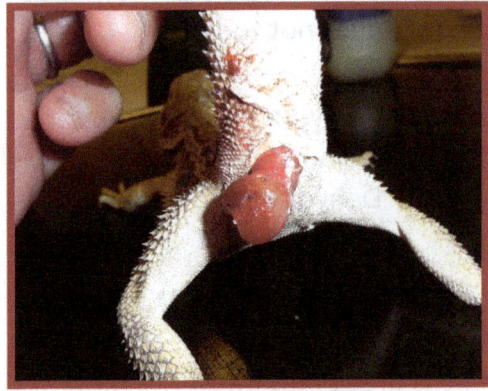

A prolapse happens when one of the organs plumbed into the vent, (for example the large intestine) gets pushed out of the body. Egg binding and a low calcium diet can cause a vent prolapse.

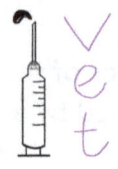

This is an emergency. If you suspect a prolapse you must take your lizard to the vet as soon as possible.

## VIRAL DISEASE

Adeno virus is a viral infection affecting mainly bearded dragons. It causes loss of appetite, diarrhoea and is very infectious.

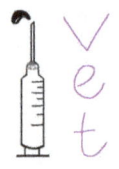

This condition needs emergency treatment by a vet.

# LUNGS

Inside the bodies of mammals there is a big sheet of muscle, called the diaphragm. This separates the chest, where the lungs are, and the abdomen, where the stomach and intestines are. Your lizard has no diaphragm. His chest and abdomen share the same space.

Partly because they have no diaphragm lizards are unable to cough. This can be a problem because if they get a build-up of fluid in their lungs, they are unable to clear it by coughing.

## LUNG PROBLEMS

### PNEUMONIA

Pneumonia is an inflammation and infection of the lungs. It is not common in lizards but can develop as a result of poor housing.

It is vital that the reptile house is kept at the correct temperature and has the correct level of humidity.

 A good diet protects the immune system.

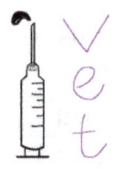 If your lizard is showing signs of illness then you must take him to the vet.

# HEART

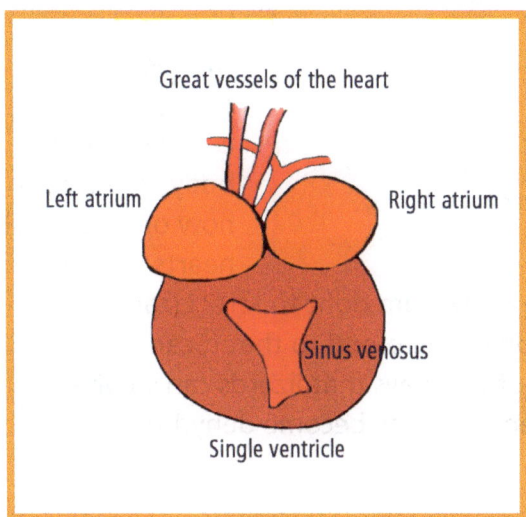

The heart is a specialised muscle which collects blood full of oxygen from the lungs and pumps it around the body. It also collects blood full of carbon dioxide from the body and pumps it back to the lungs. This cycle goes on continuously.

The heart sits in the chest cavity in mammals and is divided into four chambers. The right atrium collects blood full of carbon dioxide from the body, sends it down to the right ventricle which then pumps it to the lungs. The left atrium collects blood full of oxygen from the lungs, sends it down to the left ventricle which pumps it around the body. Blood is constantly being pumped from right to left, via the lungs and travels around the body inside a series of tubes of varying diameters. These are known as blood vessels.

The heart of a lizard differs from the heart of a mammal in several ways. It is especially adapted to suit the life of a reptile. In small lizards, the heart sits forward in the chest, between the front legs. In larger lizards, like the monitor it is further back in the chest. Inside the heart of the lizard there are three chambers; the right atrium, left atrium and the

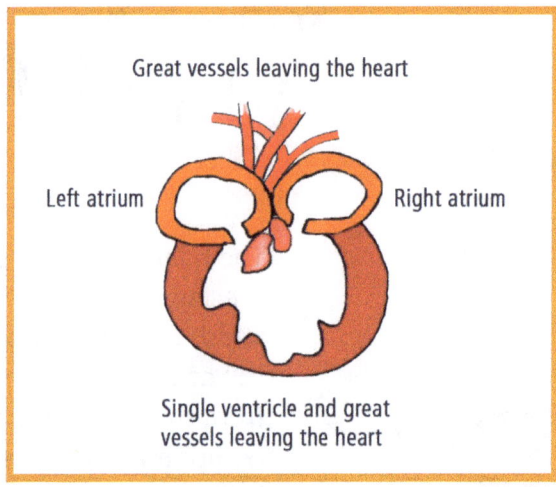

Great vessels leaving the heart

Left atrium  Right atrium

Single ventricle and great vessels leaving the heart

ventricle. There is also an extra chamber outside the heart, called the sinus venosus which collects blood. Lizards can move blood to wherever it is needed in the body. Remember how our mammal hearts always pump blood round the body from right to left? Lizards can change the direction of the blood so that it can flow backwards. This is one of the ways that lizards can survive if they are short of oxygen or if they become dehydrated.

 When a house is too cold, the heart cannot beat fast enough to keep the blood pumping to all the vital organs.

 It is vital to provide a good source of UV light and a balanced diet. The heart is a muscle and needs a constant supply of calcium to enable it to beat properly.

Heart disease is not commonly diagnosed in lizards.

# REPRODUCTIVE SYSTEM

The reproductive system is responsible for the production of sperm or eggs, mating, and the development of offspring. It varies depending on whether your lizard is male or female. Even if your lizard lives alone the reproductive system is still active and can develop problems.

Determining whether your lizard is male or female will depend on the species of lizard you have. Some lizards like the bearded dragons have obvious femoral pores. This will be a male. Females do have femoral pores but they are less prominent. With other lizard species it is much more difficult to tell the difference between male and female.

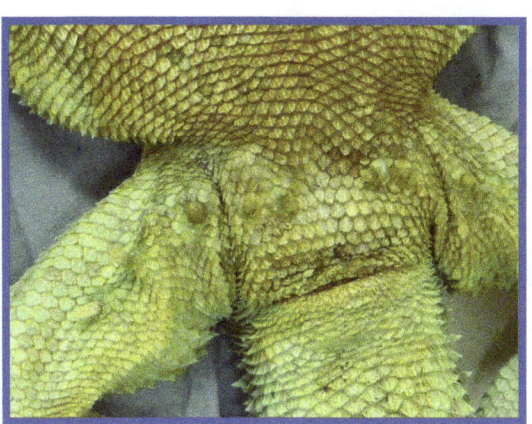

# MALES

Male lizards have two testicles which produce sperm. They are inside the body and near the kidneys. Instead of having one penis (willy) like mammals do, they have two. These are called hemipenes and are found inside the vent. Only one hemipene is used at a time for mating. The hemipenes do not carry urine the way that a mammals penis does.

# HEMIPENE PROBLEMS

## PROLAPSE

The hemipenes are normally inside the vent and only come out for mating. If a hemipene gets stuck outside the body this is known as a prolapse. A prolapsed hemipene can become damaged and infected.

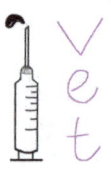

If you think your lizard has a prolapsed hemipene he needs to go to the vet. If the hemipene has suffered a lot of damage or has become infected he may need an operation to remove it.

## ABSCESS

Sometimes a hemipene can become impacted with hard pus, forming an abscess. This is a common condition in male lizards.

It is important to keep his house at the correct temperature.

 A good balanced diet will promote a healthy immune system, helping to fight infection.

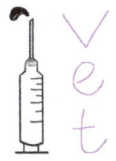 If you suspect your lizard has an abscessed hemipene you will need to take him to the vet. He may need an operation to remove the abscess or the hemipene.

Note that if a lizard does need to have a hemipene removed he will still be able to breed, as he will be able to use his other hemipene.

# FEMALES

Female lizards have two ovaries which produce eggs. They are found inside the body near the kidneys. They also have two oviducts. These are tubes along which the eggs are transported to the urodeum area of the vent. Lizards tend to lay large numbers of rubbery eggs. If they susccessfully mate with a male lizard the eggs will hatch approximately 40-60 days later, depending on the species. However, female lizards can produce eggs without mating and sometimes this can lead to problems.

# EGG PROBLEMS

## FOLLICULAR STASIS AND EGG BINDING

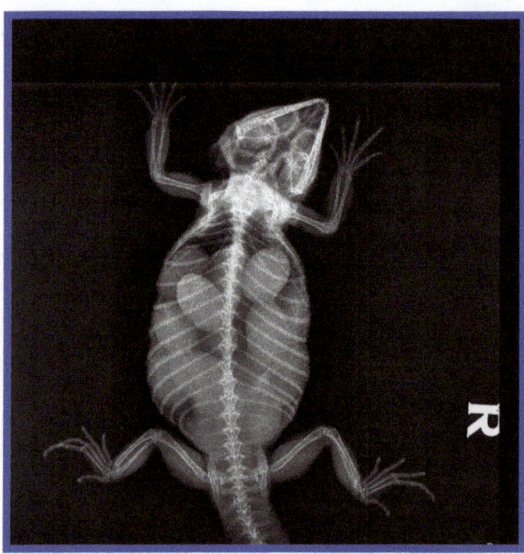

Follicular stasis is a condition where the eggs do not develop properly and are without a shell. These undeveloped eggs remain inside the body and can make an affected lizard very ill.

Egg binding is common in lizards. Here the eggs have been made and are fully developed but they become stuck inside the body and cannot be laid. The picture shows an egg bound lizard.

The house must be kept at the correct temperature. If it is too cold her body will struggle to make and lay eggs.

Dehydration will make it very difficult for your lizard to make and lay eggs.

40

Making eggs uses a large amount of energy. Ensure that your lizard has an adequate and balanced diet.

Your lizard will need a hiding place in her house with plenty of substrate. This allows her to dig holes where she will bury her eggs.

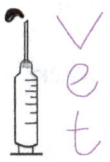
If your lizard develops any egg related problems she will need to visit the vet. Egg bound lizards need an operation to remove the retained eggs from the body. Follicular stasis can only be corrected by spaying. This is an operation to remove the ovaries and oviducts.

# KIDNEYS

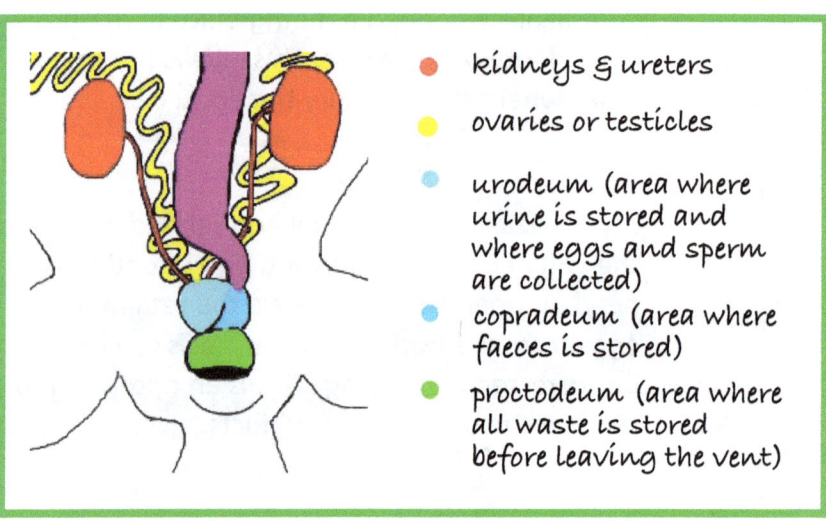

- kidneys & ureters
- ovaries or testicles
- urodeum (area where urine is stored and where eggs and sperm are collected)
- copradeum (area where faeces is stored)
- proctodeum (area where all waste is stored before leaving the vent)

Mammals and lizards have two kidneys. The purpose of the kidneys is to remove poisonous waste material from the body.

## THE MAMMAL KIDNEY

All fluid taken in by the body is processed by the kidneys. These include cups of tea, soft drinks and of course water. The kidney ensures that there is enough water to keep the body hydrated. Any water not required is stored in the bladder until it is passed as urine, which is a clear and yellow liquid.

## THE REPTILE KIDNEY

The kidney of the reptile is different as it does not have the ability to retain water within the body. Reptile urine is a mixture of water and a solid white material called uric acid. The lizard has developed unique ways to keep his body hydrated.

There is a small flap inside the urodeum that can move water into the large bowel where it is reabsorbed into the body. The lizard can also suck water up through the vent whilst bathing. Some types of the larger lizards have a bladder, but most do not. Their urine is stored in the urodeum and passes out of the body through the vent.

## KIDNEY PROBLEMS

### GOUT

Gout is a condition caused by too much uric acid in the body. The uric acid presents itself as solid white material which can easily be spotted in the urine. Sometimes these hard crystals deposit themselves in the muscles, joints and organs which can cause damage.

Make sure your lizard always has enough water to drink. Dehydration can contribute to the development of gout.

Feed a balanced nutritious diet to your lizard to prevent gout.

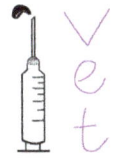

Gout is serious and will need veterinary treatment.

## KIDNEY FAILURE

Many different diseases affect the kidneys. These include infections, inflammation and toxic damage. A lizard with kidney failure will be less active than usual, lose his appetite, suffer weight loss and become dehydrated.

The house must be at the correct temperature.

Your lizard needs to have access to drinking water.

Correct diet is important. Do not be tempted to feed cat food to your lizard, as this could damage his kidneys. Do not over dust the insects with calcium powder as this can also damage the kidneys. A good diet also helps to support the immune system.

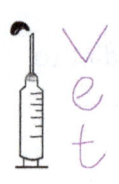

Any weight loss or change in eating habits needs a visit to the vet.

## BLADDER STONES

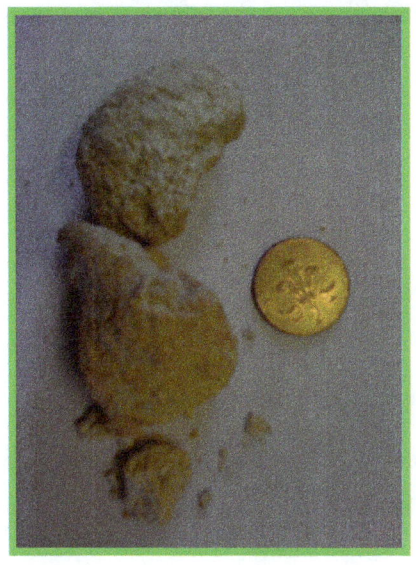

As previously mentioned, some of the larger lizards, such as the monitors have a bladder. Uric acid can collect and form into a stone which blocks the bladder. The picture shows a bladder stone removed from a Bosc monitor and a 2p coin to demonstrate the size.

The house must be at the correct temperature.

Your lizard needs to have access to drinking water.

Correct diet is important. Do not be tempted to feed cat food to your lizard, as this could damage his kidneys. Do not over dust the insects with calcium powder as this can damage the kidneys. A good diet also helps to support the immune system.

45

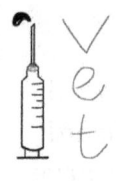 Lizards with a bladder stone will often strain to pass urine and lift their tail. Any weight loss or change in eating habits needs a visit to the vet. Bladder stones need an operation to remove them.

# NUTRITIONAL DISEASE

Nutritional diseases are caused by an incorrect diet. They can occur if fed too much or too little of the nutrients, vitamins and minerals needed to maintain good health. Nutritional disease is a common problem seen in lizards, yet it is preventable.

## MALNUTRITION

Malnutrition is a result of an incorrect diet. This may be too much or too little of any food. The photograph above shows a lizard suffering from malnutrition.

 Keeping your lizard at the correct temperature helps his stomach and small intestine to absorb all the nutrients from his food.

 Your lizard needs a good source of UV light to help his body absorb calcium from the intestine.

47

 Make sure you feed a varied diet to your lizard.

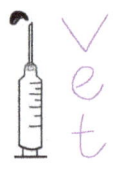 Most cases of malnutrition need specialist veterinary care.

## VITAMIN A DEFICIENCY

Vitamin A is needed to keep the insides of the mouth, the eyes and kidneys working. Lack of this vitamin can cause thickening of the eyelids, as shown in the photograph. It can also lead to kidney failure.

## VITAMIN B DEFICIENCY

Some of the larger lizards, like the Bosc monitor and tegus like to eat eggs. Too many raw eggs can lead to a vitamin B deficiency. Raw eggs contain a chemical called avidin which breaks down Vitamin B. In the wild, most eggs would be stolen from a nest and therefore would be fertile. Fertile eggs do not contain avidin.

Lizards with Vitamin B deficiency show signs of muscular weakness and tremors.

## VITAMIN D3 AND CALCIUM DEFICIENCY

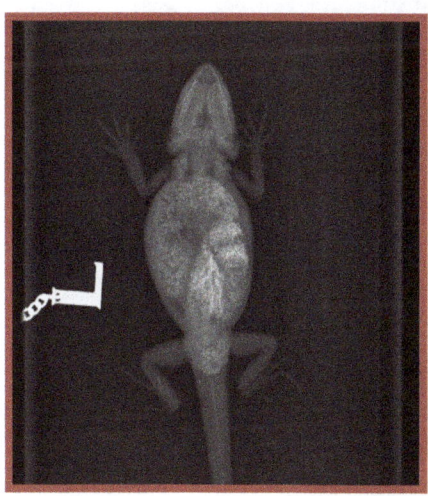

Vitamin D3 and calcium are needed to keep your lizard's bones strong and his muscles active. An insufficiency will lead to the bones becoming soft and bendy. They may even break. The lizard in the x ray has no calcium in the skeleton. The picture shows a bearded dragon with a damaged tail due to a lack of calcium in the diet.

Keeping your lizard at the correct temperature helps his stomach and small intestine to absorb all the nutrients from his food.

Your lizard needs a good source of UV light to help his body absorb calcium from the intestine.

Make sure you feed a varied diet to your lizard.

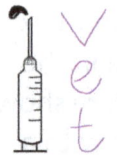
If your lizard has a nutritional disease he may have to visit the vet for vitamin injections and support with feeding.

# PARASITES

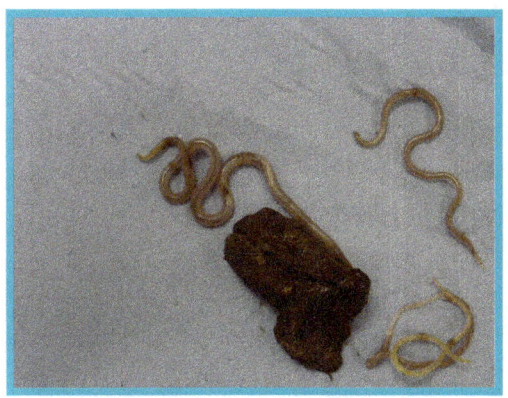

Parasites are creatures that feed off another animal. There are two basic types of parasites. Internal parasites live inside the body. External parasites live on the outside.

One example of an internal parasite is roundworm as seen in the photograph above. Roundworms and tapeworms are found inside the intestines. Mites and ticks are external parasites that suck the blood and bite the skin.

Lizards are also prone to infections by a single celled organism called coccidia. This lives within the intestine and causes diarrhoea.

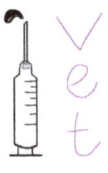

If you see any moving black or red dots on your lizard's skin, or worms in his faeces, you need to take him to the vet. These are signs of parasites.

## INFECTIOUS DISEASE

There are a number of viruses that can affect lizards. Fortunately these are not common. Irido virus is carried by insects and can sometimes make lizards unwell. Buying captive bred lizards and choosing holiday accommodation carefully reduces the risk of infection.

Bacteria and fungus can also be infectious.

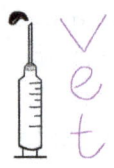

Infections need treatment from a vet. Act quickly if you have a collection of reptiles to try and prevent spreading.

# GROWTHS, TRAUMA & AUTOTOMY

## GROWTHS

This photograph shows a swelling on the end of a bearded dragon's tail.

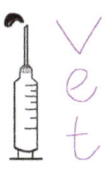

If you find any lump or swelling on your lizard take him to the vet. To find out exactly what the growth is the vet may need to do some tests. It might be a tumour and some tumours are types of cancer that can spread. However, the lumps may be abscesses or cysts. Some growths can be surgically removed.

# TRAUMA

The lizard in the 1st picture was attacked by a Bosc monitor. The x ray shows the broken bones in the jaw and the metal frame used to fix it. The last picture shows the metal frame.

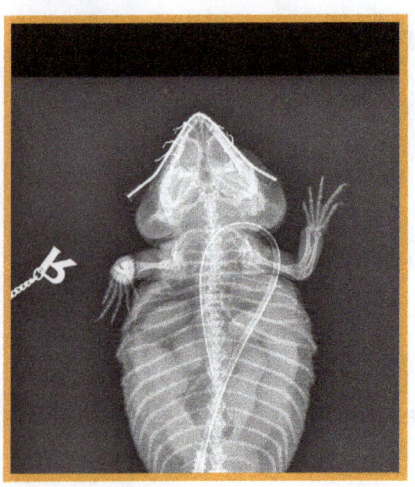

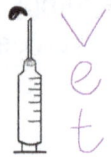

If your lizard has suffered any trauma or injury he must be taken to the vet to be checked and to receive any necessary treatment.

# AUTOTOMY

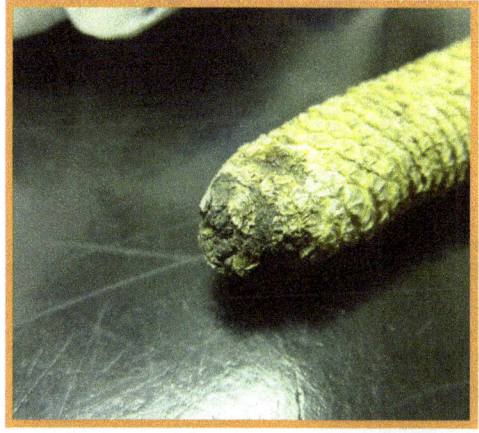

Autotomy is the ability to drop or shed the tail. A lizard can do this if he is handled roughly or if he feels threatened. The tail will eventually grow back, but it will usually be smaller. It will also be a slightly different colour.

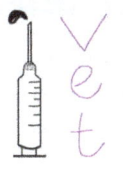 Any serious injuries need to be checked by the vet

# NEUROLOGICAL DISEASE

The brain and the spinal chord in lizards are similar to those found in mammals.

## LOW CALCIUM (HYPOCALCAEMIA)

Low calcium in the diet can cause muscular tremors. Sometimes called 'piano playing', the toes are seen to twitch when the rest of the body remains still.

## VITAMIN B DEFICIENCY

Some of the larger lizards like the Bosc monitor like to eat eggs. Too many raw eggs can cause a vitamin B deficiency. Raw eggs contain a chemical called avidin which breaks down Vitamin B. In the wild most eggs would be stolen from a nest and therefore be fertile. Fertile eggs do not contain avidin.

Lizards with Vitamin B deficiency show signs of muscular weakness and tremors.

  Ensure the house is warm to help the digestion process of food.

 It is vital to have a good quality UV bulb at the correct distance to maximise calcium absorption.

A good balanced diet, with calcium and vitamin supplements is essential to make sure the muscles work correctly.

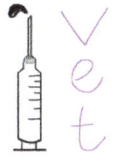
A Low calcium condition needs regular calcium injections.

## PARIETAL EYE (THIRD EYE)

Lizards have an unusual feature on the top of the head. It looks like a slightly larger scale between the eyes. This is called the parietal eye and is made up of an eye lens which is attached to an area of the brain called the pituitary gland. This 'eye' cannot see but does detect changes in light and this helps the lizard to know the best time to breed.

# INDEX

**A**

abdomen  33
abscesses  15
adeno virus  32
anus  26
atrium  35
autotomy  53, 55

**B**

bacteria  1, 4, 15, 20
bladder  42, 43, 45, 46
blood vessels  35
brain  56, 57
burns  17

**C**

calcium  10, 12, 18, 32, 36, 44, 45, 47, 49, 50, 56, 57
cancer  53
carbon dioxide  35
chambers  35
choana  26
coccidia  51
conjunctivitis  23
coprodeum  27
cornea  24
cough  33
cysts  53

**D**

diaphragm  33
digestive system  26
dysecdysis  14

## E

egg binding 32, 40
eggs 12, 20, 27, 37, 39, 40, 41, 42, 49, 56
eyelids 22, 23, 24, 48

## F

faeces 27, 30, 42, 51
fatty liver disease 29
follicular stasis 40, 41
fungus 52

## G

gout 43
growth 14, 53

## H

heart 9, 35, 36
hemipene 38, 39
hepatic lipidosis 29
hypovitaminosis a 24

## I

impaction and constipation 30
internal parasites 51
intestines 9, 26, 30, 31, 33, 51
irido virus 52
iris 22

## K

kidney failure 44, 48
kidneys 38, 39, 42, 44, 45, 48

## L

liver 27, 28, 29
lump 53

## M
mites 20
mouth 18, 26, 27, 28, 29, 48
mouth rot 28

## N
neurological disease 56
nutritional disease 50

## O
oesophagus 27
ovaries 39, 41, 42
oxygen 35, 36

## P
pancreas 27, 28
parasites 4, 51
parietal eye 57
penis 38
pneumonia 33
proctodeum 27, 42
prolapse 32, 38

## R
reproductive system 37
roundworms 51

## S
scleral ossicles 22
shedding (ecdysis) 14
sinus venosus 36
skin 10, 13, 14, 15, 17, 18, 20, 22, 51
sperm 27, 37, 38, 42
spinal chord 56
stomach 26, 27, 33, 47, 50
stomatitis 28

## T

tapeworms  51
testicles  38, 42
ticks  51
trauma  24, 25, 54
tumour  53

## U

ulcer  24
uric acid  43
urine  27, 38, 42, 43, 46
urodeum  27, 39, 42, 43

## V

vent  26, 27, 32, 38, 39, 42, 43
ventricle  35, 36
virus  52
vitamin A  18, 48
vitamin D3  49

## W

willy  38

www.ingramcontent.com/pod-product-compliance
Lightning Source LLC
Chambersburg PA
CBHW070426080426
42450CB00030B/1554